Wakefield Press

ALTERNATIVE HOLLYWOOD ENDING

Heather Taylor-Johnson is a multi-form writer living and working on Kaurna land near Port Adelaide. She's had poems published in various *Best of Australian Poetry* anthologies, and the anthology she edited, *Shaping the Fractured Self: Poetry of Chronic Illness and Pain*, was the winner of the *Mascara* Avant Garde Award. Her essays have won *Island*'s Nonfiction Prize and been shortlisted for *ABR*'s Calibre Prize, while her novel *Jean Harley was Here* was shortlisted for the Readings Prize for New Fiction. She's an arts critic and honorary title holder at the J.M. Coetzee Centre for Creative Practice at the University of Adelaide.

Alternative Hollywood Ending

poems

Heather Taylor-Johnson

Wakefield
Press

Wakefield Press
16 Rose Street
Mile End
South Australia 5031
www.wakefieldpress.com.au

First published 2022

Copyright © Heather Taylor-Johnson, 2022

All rights reserved. This book is copyright. Apart from any fair dealing for the
purposes of private study, research, criticism or review, as permitted under
the Copyright Act, no part may be reproduced without written permission.
Enquiries should be addressed to the publisher.

Typeset by Michael Deves, Wakefield Press

ISBN 978 1 74305 962 3

 A catalogue record for this
book is available from the
National Library of Australia

 Wakefield Press thanks
Coriole Vineyards for
continued support

For my American sisters and brothers

Contents

WHAT IF I WRITE A POEM? _____ 1

WHAT WE THINK OF WHEN WE THINK OF THE EARTH

WHAT WE THINK OF WHEN WE THINK OF THE EARTH_____ 4

MAN & MAN, MAN & APE, APE & APE & WOMEN_____ 5

MOTION / STASIS _____ 6

BEARS_____ 7

CLOSE TO HOME_____ 8

ON PUGET SOUND _____ 10

THE ICE _____ 11

THE HARVEST _____ 12

LAST LEG_____ 13

TOWARD PAK OU _____ 14

FEET _____ 15

BOTANIC PARK _____ 16

WHEN I COME HOME _____ 17

THUMP

THUMP _____ 19

THERE ARE SMALL ARMIES _____ 20

THE LAST WORD_____ 22

MOAB _____ 24

CRIME AND PUNISHMENT 1866 AND 2018 _____ 28

ANOTHER DANGED MIGRAINE_____ 30

THE WALL_____ 31

WHILE WE WERE SLEEPING JUST AFTER WE KISSED
WHEN THE POTUS WAS TWEETING ABOUT HIS DICK _____ 32

SICK-ASS LOVE

SICK-ASS LOVE_____ 34

TRYING TO WRITE ABOUT MÉNIÈRE'S _____ 36

SHOOT _____ 38

THIS SUMMER, WITH VERTIGO _____ 40

MOTHER GOES TO SHOPS FOR SOCCER SOCKS _____ 42

BLIZZARDS, EVERYWHERE_____ 43

THREE WAYS TO WRITE ABOUT CANCER_____ 44

    1. FREEFALL

    2. WHAT HAPPENED OVER THE WEEKEND

    3. WE WERE ALL IN LOVE WITH TESSIE

YOUR BODY IS A CASINO _____ 49

BAROMETRIC PRESSURE CHANGES _____ 50

THE WEATHER _____ 51

A USEFUL BODY

A USEFUL BODY _____ 54

SAFETY _____ 57

A DISTRIBUTION OF BLOOD _____ 58

NO LONGER A 10 (OR 'FUCK YOU, TRUMP')_____ 59

SOUS CHEF _____ 60

REFUGE _____ 61

NOT A SONNET ABOUT GOLFING _____ 62

TRANSLATION_____ 63

FRANZ SCHUBERT & GEORGIE FAME LYING DOWN TOGETHER INSIDE OF ME   64

KISS _____ 66

ALWAYS EVERYTHING _____ 74

ACKNOWLEDGEMENTS _____ 75

WHAT IF I WRITE A POEM?

What if I'm afraid? What if the tree's shadow
takes up the entire backyard? What if *white*
didn't sound like *right*? What if I ride my bike home
after the film? What if I book it in?

What if I don't want to? What if I say no?
What if I finish the bottle of wine? What if my stomach
hangs over my spandex? What if all the aeroplanes
fall from the sky? What if the wood is too heavy?

What if there weren't any cracks, ever? Or vowels?
What if I stop buying ham? What if I buy pads
instead of tampons? What if I watch only SBS?
What if I close my legs and sleep? What if I listen to you?

What if America implodes in the biggest display of fireworks
the world has ever seen? At 12:34, what if all the clocks
stop? What if I use my fingers to count? What if my boy
asks for a Nerf gun? What if my girl shoots him with it?

What if all the doors close, I stop swimming,
laughter starts tasting like old gum, I say no,
let grass grow, sweep the floor with my knitted socks?
What if I complete the crossword in my head?

What if I don't know what to do with my hair?
What about the factories? What if I haven't paid enough?
What if you called me Doctor? What if the mug only held water?
What if I take a bath? What if there was no word for *clean*?

What if everyone stopped what they were doing and sang
'There is a Rose in Spanish Harlem?' What if I eat soup
for a week? Or roses? Or ghettos? What if I read a novel a day?
What if we camp on Kangaroo Island? What if I say yes?

WHAT WE THINK OF
WHEN WE THINK OF THE EARTH

WHAT WE THINK OF WHEN WE THINK OF THE EARTH

We were here before our bodies, tiny concepts
shining through fissures, our future breaths
humming in the cold air, the earliest form
of electricity. We didn't see the breaking
of the ice but felt its horrendous blow –
why we fear death now. You say a truth
of ice is that it melts, why punish the blowtorch?
You say we should pave our way to heaven
crossing the gates in petroleum-stink
because though the angels won't approve
they'll covet our sheik black clothes.
Money doesn't grow on trees, money *is* trees
and if you cut one down, an axe through the belly,
you say it'll birth a dollar bill. I say we'll miss green:
what we think of when we think of the earth.

MAN & MAN, MAN & APE, APE & APE & WOMEN

– After reading the works of JM Coetzee

I have a fear of ancient grand narratives, like building power
with impotence. It's *morethanwhole* at heads with *lessthanwhole*,
the life of a plastic bag & the death of a bricklayer. When the truck
gains speed without a driver it's hyperbole of movement & we're long
past Satanism now. Welcome to Humankindism, psychic catastrophe,
the iron clawing the giant clam, not to mention the cows or potoroos.
We're homorapians, the haves having the havenots by the hair, business
as usual, dog eat dog, paper covers graffitied rock: 'PROSPERITY
THEOLOGY RULZ'. Did you know emotionally intelligent people
are more likely to swear? In another fucking study they laid out statistics
for smiles per kilometre. It seems we're a fairly happy society full of dead
canaries in coalmines, mostly in FNQ. How do we fill up on emptiness
& preserve ourselves through shame? What place does art have
when publicity's the currency of our time? When I typed *To be is to be
perceived* into Google Maps, I was directed to the heart of the country.
Apparently there's a market for reassurance but Google Maps has yet
to locate it. Locate these: the Juukan Gorge, the southern cassowary,
every ember on summer's rush. All you need is love   & air.

MOTION / STASIS

The other side of happiness is where the hard work's done.
Yesterday it was a beetle on its back, I didn't want to touch it
so I dragged its struggle inside of me instead, and the statue
of a woman's head with resting eyes lying sideways in our garden,
it tipped over months ago and I can't bring myself to set it upright.
Each small drama bleeds into the daily grind – I sweep this one
into the corner, I pour that one down the drain.

At the train station I hide my face in poetry, nearby bodies distracting.
I can't believe anyone's different from me, dragging around their business
wherever they go. Dear old man with the small suitcase, beige pants
and bowler hat, sometimes I think you're a paedophile, then I feel guilty.

I'm so full of anger I see angels buying tickets to cry
on the Outer Harbor line: five dollars and forty cents,
they really pack them in. I once read a story about a man
who jumped in front of a train, the driver having to drag
his body with her every day. I'm entitled to hurt, allowed to wonder
what the body might have felt like under the wheels, the other side
of happiness where pain leaves slug trails staining the wet grass.
All day I pull at the pain like weeds, try to loosen the roots
so it might lift completely from the mire. It's motion at least. Stasis.

BEARS

– after Libby Hart's 'Stag'

Hold tight – there are bears in our yard
out front of the home that hardly contains
our running bodies and pot-belly stove
the pantry full of spaghettios, sock-décor
plastic toys – it's magic.

I tell my son to hold still, no snow crunch
no twig crack or questions, just that mama
and her curious cub rutting and lolling
in front of us, our yard, our house, our
very own breath vaporising into their
air, their tree bark and weed stalk.

CLOSE TO HOME

This lake says *oofta*, something my Minnesotan
mother might say while walking bent-over uphill
or something that I might say while dusting books
for years untouched, the ashy stories flying straight
into my eyes and blinding me with their language.
Mine's a quieter *oofta* than hers, though equally substantial.

Because I want to be in lakes or on them or by them
how had I missed this an hour out of the city's symmetry?
Oofta, a gentle shock gushing forth, the lake like us
in our earlier years growing out of desperate sex
and swimming deeper, where less words needed saying
though when we spoke we saw bubbles.

I love you today, as if you were a lake.

Minnesota is a lakeland where I drank Dr Pepper
while drying in the sun, my young body growing
and endless, a photograph stored in a shoebox
in my parents' closet in Florida, where children
lecture adults through megaphones
     guns are bad / guns are bad / guns are bad
and they should know.

The day before we left for the lake I picked up our son
at the usual spot, the shade of the gumtree still
near the roundabout, the couch still by the crooked mailbox
outside the brittle house – not everything had changed

in the two hours since I'd heard the news of the school shooting:
my son's backpack still like a shell on top of his long and skinny legs,
his skin so white, his eyes so large – not everything had changed.

The bottle from the last winery on the way to this lake
is still cold as we toast the lake while watching the lake
baptise itself again and again. No train schedules here.
Here, there are twigs to gather. No local pubs.
Only purple swamphens in the reeds.

Tell me you feel the ripple too – a leaf fallen by the breeze,
a dog's bark shaking the surface of the lake and the *oofta* vibration
that it makes, an oar lifted by our son coaxing out the water's words,
like uncovering a memory then stowing it again.

The lake hears our stories too, drowns in every one.

ON PUGET SOUND

– for Paula

For now, water
the way it lays pain down on the blue horizon
where your child's face is rip-lit, reflecting off your own
        keeping him near.

Because death lingers
in the quiet mourning of every evening
you do what you must, in the smallest way
        and sometimes it is water.

Just water for now
while there's still a bit of sun. Soon a chill will fall,
your knees curling up to warm your breast, where the heart rests
        between its tiny aching beats.

Not far from the ships' heaving
your body feels a kindred thing, hauling itself through the tides.
Thirsty birds dip their beaks into the traces of your grief
        then fly away, over water.

THE ICE

The ice is in the water, though no water that's known my skin where
I dove into waves and jellyfish teased the bubbles of my wake or
where I entered from a wooden dock, maybe my ankle rolling on
a deeply polished river rock, or in water where a group of us in our
twenties tried not to look at each other's naked bodies or maybe
when I floated on my back, found language in the water's hushing
vowels – this ice is something new.

This water is something new to me, the ice curving inward and the
water smoothing its slow chip, the way a hand might a lover's hip,
a basic need for speechlessness, *I love you* lapping at the ice, water
tonguing millions of years, our life and the life of the ice, a balance
impossible without death and threaded tightly with mood – the ice
is kissing the air.

The ice is kissing the guide's skin, the guide who's fished it from the
water, the guide who holds it high, like a sacrifice, eating the ice as if
it's meat breaking apart in his mouth, softening as he salivates and
he passes it to us so that we might hold and understand cold, the ice-
slivers and ice-sting (it was melting *anyway*, had broken *regardless*)
and we pass it around, taste it and waste it and once we've felt it
on our tongues and swallowed the place into our bodies someone
throws what's left of the ice back into the water – the ice is now
smaller in the water.

THE HARVEST

Dig in the dirt, this Earth's wreckage we hold
in our blood, it is between our toes, cannot shower
the dirt from our hair, we pick the fine grains of it
from between our teeth, we muddy ourselves silly.

Look how the queen rogue pumpkin blooms,
a bell-framed Madonna, her colour curving
like a healthy breast – she rests too fat
from her proud insides to be shaken by any wind.

We know the garden teaches us green as it teaches us
water, and death comes in stalks that crumble to dirt
and dirt is a living spectacle, we know there is weight
because of shape, because the soil will regurgitate

and there is only one small table between us
                              and it is loaded with food.

LAST LEG

Oh my love, what have we done
sealing ourselves inside these black gates
with nothing but the sea, the millipedes,
the tour groups posing in the sand
and the old men golfing, all of us
counting days in purple currency
and the crabs, translucent at our toes –
one is crawling across this very poem.
Here is my coconut water.
(Where is your lager?)
Gone are the golden temples
and twelve year-old monks
the beggars' children, the moped children
our own ones staring and searching for recognition.
We've traded tuk-tuks for shuttle buses
dirty rivers for waves that swallow
then spit us out. Yesterday a plastic bag
filled with tar washed up on the shore
by the yellow umbrellas where we sat
eating meat on a stick. The cleaner
leaves us a new bottle of water every afternoon.

TOWARD PAK OU

Trust in the current of this slow brown river to carry you through the day.
Follow bamboo floating by like the future, both with purpose and without.

Know that beyond the mountains are more, and the same river,
its plastic-bag baubles and white birds.

Villagers wave you on your way, wearing the river like old and worn
sandals, like shorts that slip to their hips, like shade across their shoulders.

FEET

Ancient stones stomp mossy on wet earth, then hold.
Ghosts slide through the cracks headfirst, trying to drag
down the walls with their long toenails.
I trip over cobblestone in Velcro sandals.

It's hard to find your feet in a foreign country where packs
of people, two walking poles each like four-footed beasts, echo
through the dales, vibrating heather in the ears of the sheep
and the grumbling clouds and the hanging bough.

How many colours of green have I seen? *Here*
here therethere here. Indulgence is this,
and sometimes a morning bath (or just a bath),
hot chocolate in a castle when you can't dry your shoes.

Shadows by gravestones are colder than the day-long dew.
Under the tree I see a worm trying to dig to the dead.
Then the clouds hide the sun and I lay down, imagining
how the worm and the dead must feel, neither having a foot to stand on.

At the pub, everyone's talking about the Butter Tubs
and three pints into it, so are we. Nearly legless,
which would also mean footless,
how will we ever walk away?

BOTANIC PARK

My son asks what colour is the sky and I say blue – *just look at it, what a beautiful blue* – and we stop and stare into the sky, see different things like the future (*him*) and the past (*me*).

He says 'black' for a universe of reasons including atmosphere, prisms and an astronaut who's been there and knows it all.

I tell him black doesn't suit Adelaide's peachy veins in the bloodshot eyes of a lazy summer's sunset, even with the pump and grind of black tyres, black roads and the burnt black crumbs waiting for me on our oven's wire racks.

Black magpies cawk about their many white patches and I fear for my unborn grandchildren who will one day ask what colour is the sky and I'll say *just look at it, that rusty rust-colour!*

We're on a blanket and I've brought a picnic, we're by the river – can you smell that river? – a sixty-year-old rock legend is about to sing, we're a lucky country, the grass smell, the river stink, the waft of a joint; somewhere a child is eating Shapes.

Soon the sun will set, its sinking felt first on the crowns of our heads. My son will ask *What time will we go home?* and I will say *When it is dark and the sky is glittered with light* because that's what it looks like in the black of night.

WHEN I COME HOME

Imagine it, the sun spread under the skin of the lake,
water bugs scattering like they've got a plan,
my middle son rising in gold and ripple.

Let's reel it in, call it life for the duration of my stay.

                    Out there it's a bumper-sticker state
                    but my patriotism doesn't drive down I-75
                    switching lanes like cursors on the net,
                    clicking and breaking and zooming past,

                    hatred disseminating that fast.

For citronella candles and bottles of beer, for algae and bass
and copper pipes, for the stars that are maps to my children's
nights – when I come home let's stay at the lake.

The fires we light will be art for art's sake.

THUMP

THUMP

Tremendous mouth it
aims at the belly
& the just as important
likewise tough grey
matter I call *Mine*

> We won't parade one without the other
> > we won't 'parade' at all

> Know that there are sinkholes
> > bracing themselves
> > > for our stampede

> > > > My daughter knows your name,
> > > > I've said it like a catch-phrase
> > > > hurled against the red wall –
> > > > > sounded like *thump*

Words are water
we can let them draw a tepid bath
or *monsoonthisshitfuckennow!*

> > > 'Child, if ever there was a time to swear –'

> > I look to my own mother
> > her endless movement & ripple

> her fight wasn't planned or talked about;
> > feminism hung around her neck
> > > like an iron sling

But it's true things are better now

> > > It's true that things are the same.

THERE ARE SMALL ARMIES

Words borrowed from 'America the Beautiful' written by Katharine Lee Bates

Oh beautiful, there are small armies in my America of gracious skies
of spacious skies and cans that are made from aluminium,
there are small armies of erratics who wave lean sacks of amber
grain
and refuse to be put on hold, blaming ethnic minorities for their
burnt toast
and littering death stares and more cans over the purple the blue
the verdant mountains, small armies of men who've yet to consider
that blood is no warmer when touching death because death is so
unnaturally
cold, small armies of thick-booted feet trampling through fruited
plains
in time with arms mere bone and skin, the hate-tendrilled bridges
to some God's oblivion, and there won't be any shedding-grace,
not in this place, America. If you see these armies of brotherhood
rising
barricade yourself in a toilet stall immediately. So many guns that
the chests
of the men are turning into metal, their heads are turning into
metal,
someone should take a blowtorch to them growing in the streets, at
the doughnut
shops, inside bus stations where junkies beg, in front of malls where
women

wearing sunglasses drop to the ground. They're all over the joint, their pilgrim
feet at rest stops and schools – *there is an army in every school* – these men
who appear to be mechanics and stockbrokers and bartenders from the wide
wilderness and skyscrapered land, teenagers with acne and ill-fitting coats.
Once I heard children sing in a choir 'confirm thy soul'; it's a good thing
we finally stopped blaming rock n roll. When I was a child there were sightings
of these armies, but rare, like babies found in abandoned cars by heroes
of liberating strife, or toddlers stolen from gorillas in a zoo enclosure –
rare but there, country-loved and hate-dribble, more small armies
than we could've known, waiting, yes, and they'll keep on waiting as they stand
outside the security gates of our future memorials to the shot-up Americans, oh
the beautiful, waiting with their angry steady fingers cocked, gold refine, grain
divine, but they won't be allowed in. Instead we'll see them in the fireworks
each 4th of July, the gleaming streams carrying their alabaster spirits
undimmed by human tears. We'll see their ghostly faces blossoming
in brilliant shards of night sky glass – I would *ooo* and *ahhh* if I wasn't so scared.
How do we stop them, the age old question? Take to the streets and demand
their speech be washed down the sewers by a high-powered pressure hose?
That's wet language, look at their wet bodies coming out of the sea
the shining sea. They're trying to sing their anthem louder than I sing
my poem. Should I sing it louder? *Oh beautiful for blood-stained eyes …*

The armies aren't small at all.

THE LAST WORD

Even a race to Obama, she was gonna beat Obama. I don't know who would be worse, I don't know, how could it be worse? But she was going to beat – she was favored to win – and she got schlonged, she lost, I mean she lost.   – Trump

I.

A muscle of a thing, sends forth and sires
     armies of them   *millions*
     shooters and looters and rulers.

Wants movement and darkness
     the damp smell that will see it home.

2.

    shlonged: to whack with a penis
Hold the penis – blood-driven – with two hands
so that your hands are filled with yourself,
and then your body, filling with yourself,
until you're finally full of yourself
so that there are armies, *millions*
and then whack her hard.
shlonged: to fuck with a penis
Push the penis – risen in a brouhaha –
into the whispers of her cave
where time sits and contemplates,
then make with the looting
and shooting and blast yourself
into her moon and slip out, spent   and sleep.

3.
The muscle in instinct

      of looting and siring

         the armies of millions

         wants darkness and damp

      home and cave to contemplate

shambolically   then sleep

4.
Not tonight.
No.

MOAB

Patti Smith read Footnote to Howl on our first night
at Blues Fest, threw the poem on the floor & spat –

      holy punk & common cold thick with holy mucus

She didn't sing People Have the Power
but recited it as a giant poem

      Patti Smith was a giant poem

We screamed – everyone was screaming
like when Buddy Guy played guitar with his *ass*
& when Buffet came on, how we realised
that Parrot Heads are global

      (my parents in Florida are Parrot Heads
      we sent them a photo of the screaming crowd)

Bonnie Raitt sang the night
Trump dropped the 21,000-pound bomb
she was sexy at seventy, smiled sideways
   slid those strings
     like they were broken hearts
      having a hoedown at a bar & grill

She was mad as hell – everyone was
because the world had to bear witness
to Donald Trump & after the bomb

      there was no turning back

It was our fifteenth anniversary
we were babies though we sagged
& cracked, slept in our tent
touching through the cold night

holy snaking legs & arms

In the morning we woke to pounding propellers
aeroplanes dropping skydivers
parachutes disappearing behind tree-line

For breakfast we had egg & bacon rolls
at jacked-up festival prices
because we didn't want to cook

& fair enough, it'd been a hard six months –

Bonnie Raitt could've written our soundtrack
Patti Smith could've written a poem

holy women of the word

Love chips away, but sometimes you wonder
how much of the chipping is us & how much
is the wearing down of the world

This was our time to mend
& when the Doobie Brothers
came on I kissed you after
every song

We were free, privilege so webbed
between our fingers and toes
we swam through the audience

> *holy water holy waves*
> *holy holy*
> *school of fish*

Each time we found our perfect view
it felt like the universe was making room for us

> & I think it happened in every tent

Who could blame us for being confused
thinking Afghanistan was *so 2001*, history the silence
after war, the contemplation we then turn into song

The night of the GBU-43 we were drunk on ten-dollar beer
Mavis Staples sang *March Up Freedom Highway*
> 2017 not '63 still she's rasping

> *whole world is wonderin*
> *what's wrong with the United States*

> Trump's Mother of All Bombs
> spent in an Afghan grave

We hated that they were calling it the MOAB
because we'd camped in the thick
of Moab's red-rocks, slipping each day
in heaven's clay, washing it off in the Colorado
& when we laughed in the canyon, it echoed

>   *Holy bliss, holy gladness*
>   *holy holy*
>   *joy*

Moab demanded our respect, not the other way around
like Bonnie Raitt & Buddy Guy & Rhiannon Giddens
(I cried when she sang about flying away)

Music makes sense of our world
made better sense of our marriage
than we'd been doing since November's election

& here it was April, in love again
so we talked about returning in another five years

   swatted away what-ifs like we were doing the shag

>   *death, somehow*
>   *not even an option.*

CRIME AND PUNISHMENT 1866 AND 2018

I was aiming for genius
starving, febrile, I dreamt
of a horse being flogged & fallen

I am aiming for genius
bloated & tanned, I dream
of shooting a lion dead

life was always about death
when it wasn't about living

life is always about money
when it isn't about sex

the old question: you're standing   on a precipice   only big enough
for you –   what would you do   alone in dark storms   until the end of time
            & the abyss below   live or die?

the horse hadn't a choice

the lion hasn't a chance

nor the woman I called *Louse*

nor the person I call *Woman*

I had an axe in my coat
& the drowning – what was that?

I have an army at my feet
& the storms – what are those?

wretchedness everywhere
in the river, in a closet, my sheets
wet & I ate only bread

wretchedness everywhere
in the river, in a closet, my sheets
silk & I eat a lot of burgers

I literally threw money into the wind
& stuffed it into strangers' hands

I literally throw money at skyscrapers
& stuff it into Russia's hands

or gave it to the widow of the man
whose face was disfigured
by horses' hooves & wheels
horses again, so many horses

or give it to the widow of the man
whose face was mutilated
by an AR-15 semi-automatic
guns again, so many guns

because my clothes
were stained & frayed
I knew the woman had been raped

I drank on an empty stomach
wrote an article about Napoleon

my best friend was frantic
wouldn't leave me alone & everyone
answered to three names –
no wonder I was confused

my girlfriend gave me her Bible
& I thought I was meant to convert
but was God about living or dying
because that could've influenced
my decision

it's true misery multiplied

there was a suicide by the watchtower

a consumptive's blood
in a yellowed hanky

they imprisoned me in Siberia.

because my clothes
are tailor-made
I know that women claim rape

I've never had an empty stomach
tweet about Kim Jong-un

my enemies are frantic
won't leave me alone & everyone
answers to me –
no wonder the world is confused

my model wife gave me her son
& I'm going to be a God for him
but is God about creation or destruction
because that could influence
my style

it's true money multiplies

there are racial jokes in the private jet

protesters' bloodstains
on the street

I holiday at Mar-a-Lago.

ANOTHER DANGED MIGRAINE

Father of my son's friend wants a Trumped-up t-shirt straight from
America & I've (*what?*) suggested Appalachia as a place for my family
to gather, the state of Georgia where in 1992 a former grand wizard of
the ku klux klan made a run for president and got the vote though the
north Georgia mountains, it must be told, are beautiful this time of year:
chicken-yellow, Sunkist-orange & blood-red-running.

Guns kill people *guns* kill people, my heart no longer beating a straight
line. It's possible one can feel at home & be a stranger & feel strange & be
at-home, fear growing stronger with age, like cellulite & moles.

Leader 1 says his penis is bigger than the missile that belongs to Leader
2 so they whip out their weapons of mass destruction & play with their
light sabres like *whack! whack!* not even considering that my vagina
mass-created three separate times, so take *that!* and *that!* and *that!*

The mountains aren't to blame. Who is to blame? Even I have a soft spot
for my son's friend's father. Every person is unique, it's what makes life
so … *great*. It's what makes my brain incessantly ache.

THE WALL

The wall will be made of repetitive fabric, the bones and sinew
of all the Jews who look like Jews and the wide-spread fingers
of born-again palms praising the God on the 44th floor and a line
of black burqas on laundry day. It will be taller than a man
lifting a woman who we hope won't be wearing a dress.
The children building it (with their grandparents next to them)
might try to dig a trench to the other side where there will be a lemonade
stand and an old plastic ice-cream container filled with silver coins
but the children (and their grandparents) will be punished
as the earth is punished during a volcanic eruption. The wall
will be like a chastity belt separating the womb from the vagina
because one is fertile and the other dirty. The wall will be tremendous;
really big. It will be a great, great thing this wall and anyone caught
climbing it will be ridiculed for being a monkey (or an insect),
which isn't an insult, just an analogy, because monkeys (and insects)
climb walls. The wall will keep these types out: thieves and lovers
and mothers and rapists and people who can never shut up,
like our gardeners and some beauty queens and all of their pimps
and those people with angel wings tattooed on their backs.
The wall will ensure that this place, our place, continues to smell
like the wild fields on a spring day in every spray-on deodorant ad.

WHILE WE WERE SLEEPING JUST AFTER WE KISSED WHEN THE POTUS WAS TWEETING ABOUT HIS DICK

Then there is the myth of great powers
– butterflies not aeroplanes
their jagged lines
not their streams of petrol flight –
or sunlight, or lamplight
just before we kiss

take the talk and swagger away
the pendulum of a hanging fate
it was late, there were stars
a lamplight in the mist
just before we kissed

nothing matters when we sleep
nothing matters when we sleep
unless it's a dream
or a burrowing mite
the myth of every lamplight.

SICK-ASS LOVE

SICK-ASS LOVE

When you asked *is that it*
I wanted to say *there is always more*
and *no, it is never finished*
never enough rain to drown it
never enough dirt to hide in
but I was sick that year
in bed and bed (in bed and bed)
so I said *yes*, confused, fatigued
just wanting to keep things simple.

You might get tired of hearing this
but 'sick' is a word I love to use
(and 'love' too) *I am sick of this rain*
I am sick of the noise that whitegoods make
I am sick of mirrors, stuff like that
but during my year of 'interruption'
I was all *I am sick* and *you are love*
(I am you, love you sick).

That year wasn't my life
not my stroll through wildflowers
or skinny dip; not my board game.
More a deceptive plunge through a tunnel of rapids
then falling to earth, hackneyed on my ass.
I like the word 'ass' too
sick is ass and *lovesick*
(love your ass you sick-ass love).

See. It's good to recall the worst of it
because it wasn't all bad, was it?
And it definitely wasn't *it*, was it?
There was also the soft and the sleep.
There was also the hold and the keep.

TRYING TO WRITE ABOUT MÉNIÈRE'S

I.

It was a sad day when you came to realise your body would never be glamorous holding onto the spinning Earth, but did you consider it might be closer to nature than all those other conventional bodies because, like Earth, it was spinning too? Why did you say 'dizzy' when the word is like 'giddy'? Is not 'falling' more appropriate to a bottom dweller with a head that follows like a little brother or sister? Tinned tomatoes, pepperoni, soy sauce, cheeses, babaganoush bought in a plastic container and the crackers that carry it to your guilty mouth: you must avoid salt though your body craves it, being so full of the ocean. You are a lost fish. Your home is an eddy. You write about sickness in bubbles plucked from underwater screams, but it cannot be an art form if the words pop before they are written. How could anyone read them?

Too many times you've wondered: if each word is monotone, why, then, should we sing? What is it to say 'poetry saves' when bile dribble stains your favourite writing dress? Or to say you're tired of back-stroking in a circle when you close your eyes to the glaring sun? Or to say when you are sleeping in your rocking bed which rides upon waves, you yourself are dreaming that you've wrapped your body in a swinging cocoon and will emerge days later, wings and all.

2.

You've forgotten silence. You never had to put it into words because you'd always known it is the Earth's phantom limb, and you, too, have felt like that: maybe more a phantom tongue than a leg while silence was a nostril inhaling everything. Now you try to place it, throwing letters like paint on a wall, writing poems all through the untameable sky: *the soundlessness of ants / or photosynthesis of plants*. You edit relentlessly, knowing 'silence' is an uncontainable word, like 'hatred' and 'death', so best to avoid it altogether.

Still, you want to write about the sound in your left ear. You want to say it is time's drone measuring the molecules swimming past your head, or time's trick of letting loose the dam that will take you under, but it is not natural to speak without the words you've lost amidst the noise. No, none of this is natural.

3.

Once you wore a dress that fitted you perfectly. Health spilled from the top of the open neckline and below the slackened hem; your curves were so round against the silk that your body danced whenever you moved. Writing in it was like doing the rumba in your seat; sometimes ballet. Now it's like you have taken it out of the wash to find it shrunken and dripping and torn down the middle, the threads of the seams only just hanging on. When you hold it up, you see the colour has faded. As have the trees. As have the faces of your loved ones. Your favourite painting can no longer tell its story. All are shavings of dead skin filed from the memory of your earth-worn heels. Now you have a fishtail and are growing fins. You have no need of dresses because your scales would only snag the fabric. Now you are resigned to return to the place you crawled out of millions of years ago, thinking that somewhere, there must be a coral reef.

SHOOT

In hindsight
travelling through 4 hemispheres at 39,000 feet
might not have been in my body's best interest

> (Lindbergh was 25 when he
> and his plane seized the Atlantic
> & it caused quite a stir)

because my body
might have re-magnetised too quickly,
a malfunction due to rapid displacement,
toilets flushing backwards & that

> (at 25 Millie Steimer
> was the first person to be banished
> from both the USA & the USSR
> (*go hard or go home*))

though perhaps it was something less scientific –
I'd left my family & the mountains & stars that I knew,
emotionally skewing my balancing crystals

> (when Lawrence Berg won the Nobel Prize
> for ascertaining crystal structures
> he was 25)

but not for nothing I migrated here,
the man, the three babies we had,
worth getting sick at 25
so I could write a book of poems about it

                              (beloved mythologist Joseph Campbell
                                    moved to Woodstock at 25
                                     to read a ton of classics)

sometimes we have to leave our mothers
in order to become our own mothers
& kiss our own temples
to make pain go away

                              (the performance artist Chris Burden
                                       created 'Shoot' at 25
                                       & made his friend
                                    shoot him in the arm).

THIS SUMMER, WITH VERTIGO

Some things hurt;
we are all bruised.

In this body, a pretty body: my heart
                    a bloody thunderclap
                          the bones of my neck
                              like balloon strings,
                                      tethering and tethered.

When I'm not lying down
(or stretching or moving or

sitting or squatting or crouching)
                          I am standing:
                                    not quite statue, not quite tree
                                        not quite as inexhaustible
                                            as a garden shed.

Some people think that all of these words
– *I, body, tree* – are virtually the same

but because I'm also wind and wave
            so crookedly contained

                          I say to them nu-uh: with a small click
                                                        at the back of my
                                                          pretty throat.

This feeling's not the worst but if I could master re-feeling
I would choose that first summer, a dark room

my fingers searching
your thickness of hair

       transmitting these words
          from your brain to mine (so pretty) –
            life, legs, now

back when we were famished
too full to move – remember?

Our after-breath like wind, our skin like waves.
   I remember, as a summer night might:
          bedside lamp and shadow
            window open to the street
              no other feeling existing.

MOTHER GOES TO SHOPS FOR SOCCER SOCKS

Where is the book of falling – not in love, not out of it
nor from grace – just down? The book that loses balance,
that chapter about feeling ok in the shopping mall but then

there's a shiny-tiled incline leading to the sports store
& the heroine pushes her trolley up, entering another headspace
where matrons circle like paid extras *that's what it felt like*

and she's lost, not even much of an incline at all, not a hill
or metaphor steeped in anything but certainly a challenge,
like learning to walk after your legs have fallen asleep

& she's got a tilt so light & to the left you wouldn't know it
if you looked at her, that line from Dead Poet's Society
about seeing the world from a different view?

I'm not saying this isn't normal; I'm saying it is & that's the problem
I always seem to have when I'm feeling ok: one minute the reflection
in the glass is slick & honest & the next on an incline it bends.

I wonder what my eyes would look like if I was the protagonist,
that fear & surprise paired with déjà vu, the plot so mundane:
Mother Goes to Shops for Soccer Socks.

BLIZZARDS, EVERYWHERE

O life, you lofty muse, lift this woman who tilts her head towards the sun
and closes her eyes to feel it. She's near to giving up, her unrequited flirting
with you and demanding of you just too much. Your move now: wrap her legs
around your centre and raise her breath from your airy breast. It's 2019
things are grim, gunshots scaring birds away, her dog no longer barking
and though the thaw keeps promising, it never does come. It's true
everybody hurts, but while one person's pain is exquisite another's will drag
its ass in the snow. She's both of them, and more. Hold her, quick –

                    before time strolls in and ruins everything.

THREE WAYS TO WRITE ABOUT CANCER

1. Freefall

I'll try and be specific: *ocean, flight, death* –
it really is impossible. On this airplane
I am expectant and zen, you would think the two
couldn't lie together but in me they're tangled and sated.
I will arrive at my destination before I've even left.
You can see I am poised to write something big
though I will try to avoid using vast words
like *ocean*, like *flight*, like *death* even though I am serious
about the Pacific right now, amazed I see whitecaps
from 38,000 feet, and it's night. I've imagined falling,
envisaged my face crumpled in disbelief and regret
which can only look like Hollywood.
I feel like an actor so how can I be centred?
How can I know this isn't real and the ocean
won't become my eternal home? (Now *that's* a big word;
I apologise.) It is big to say I've just left my friend
ravaged with scars, lame with limp, one thin clump
of hair hanging off of her head, her bones screaming
Don't   look   at   us   like   that!
I am sorry, I was trying to help, I was trying to be a grown-up.
I was trying to remember that some things in life
are bigger than me though I don't want to overdo it.

My friend and I used to jump out of small airplanes
and I don't mean to be metaphorical at all.

I mean we strapped expensive parachutes to our backs
and flew to each other, connected and separated
and connected again, we did it over and over – it's a whole sport
and I suppose it does sound like a metaphor for friendship.
If we were lucky, we fell through a cloud and everything
disappeared. Once I got too low to the ground, disbelief
but no regrets, nothing like you see in films.
Once my friend broke her fibula leaving the strut
of a Cessna-182. I've watched it on an old video tape
dozens of times, the white-jumpsuited bottom of her leg
flapping like a flag in the wind. It was nothing like death,
like now. Now is the best and only reason I would visit Colorado
for one week at the end of winter when I feel the cold fiercely
in my fingers and toes and I hate the sound of my shaky voice
when I complain about the icy air again and again and again
and again – I am stuck on repeat, though I'm trying to rewind.

Once my friend and I were nineteen. I am not confident anymore;
I am not *hot*. I am trying not to be a narcissist or fuddy duddy.
I am trying to skip the part where my friend tells me
about her liver and lymph nodes, especially the lungs
because she cannot breathe without a tank.
I want to go back to Virginia, where we once lived.
From the sky everything was green if it wasn't sparkling water
and nothing was faultless, only lush and ours, that sky
our world, the bonfires our world, our tits the world
when we flashed them around in the hangar after we swallowed
the worm in the dregs of the tequila, and the next day we were sick.
Imagine saying 'sick' now and only half meaning it.

I am also trying to drink a bloody mary. I don't drink tequila
on airplanes, the pull-down table crowded with vodka
and tomato juice, crowded with journal and all these thoughts.
At my friend's house for a week I talked to fill in silences
when all she wanted was quiet and soft, the chemo
confusing the lines of her thinking, gnawing pathways
to important receptors. *Please* she asked *can you just not talk?*
I want to write it all down. Everything I couldn't say:
'I am middle-aged, I have children and I can't stop thinking
about them because I'm thinking about your child too.'
When I booked last-minute tickets from Adelaide to Denver
I'd considered bringing my daughter / so glad I didn't
bring my daughter. *Daughter* is a big word. And *silence.*
And *chemotherapy.* I mostly remember my friend winking at me
while we endlessly packed our parachutes. She was
silly and sexy, we were nineteen, I am stuck on repeat,
her favourite sports bra was a striped one and she's lost a breast,
she's lost her appetite but not the sass, the air that bastes
her frozen skin trying like hell to smother it.

I am trying to write an epic poem about skydiving,
I think I've been trying for twenty-five years –
will it never go away? I still dream about it
though now there is a thunderstorm, somebody has died
on the jump before mine, I've borrowed old and sketchy gear,
I've landed without a parachute. It's different, but I still
wake up to that pure sense of freefall which my friend
and I talked about whenever she felt strong enough
to cope with reminiscing. It's the kind of feeling

that never goes away. Sometimes, when I'm stuck
on my bicycle behind a truck, I smell Cessna-182s.
I am in love with airplanes, old or new, small or big
this one carrying me backwards through time zones
and far away from my friend. It'd be nice to sleep
over the next seven hours but I don't want to forget.
I'm trying to get it all down and it's really only about one thing
that I don't want to mention and all that is attached to it,
like imagining a treasure in a shipwreck on the ocean's floor:
where would I begin the gathering and how could I raise
it to the surface? Once I wrote an entire book on death
and wanted my friend to read it, but she'd just gotten sick
when it came out and sending it to her seemed cruel.

Everything is cruel: the fact that birds fly through propellers
and I'm toasting it with vodka, the fact that I'm trying to write
while strangling the planet with carbon emissions from jet fuel
and it's likely I've just seen my friend for the last time.
It's impossible, so many problems in this world
and none of them are mine. My friend's problem isn't even mine
though I'm trying to claim it – do you see what I've done?
I can't stop life from being about me. I am trying to imagine
what it would be like to know that your parachute
is not going to open before you hit the ground,
something we both used to think about before we jumped,
unlike global warming and dead birds. I would open the door
and look out the plane for the place where I wanted to land
and ask myself why was I doing this, why all the risk?
Then I'd be hooting and swooping, flying to my friend,
extra points for a kiss pass. I am trying I am trying to rewind.

2. *What happened over the weekend*

Clouds ghosted the lake, a moonlight haze, while inside
my lover and I, still drunk and post-coital, had woken
in each other's arms to an all-out wind. Outside, a spark
had multiplied and travelled far and when we rose,
across the lake, the trees were blazing, the smoke charging
the sky like some beautiful despot waging a private war.
We stood naked at the window, the lights out, felt everyone
in the bay must be doing the same, all two hundred of us stunned
by a respectful calm, by a new dread, the fire in front of us
hungering and devouring night. We followed headlights
down the dirt road until they stopped, their steady rays facing off
a glorious inferno. How can someone get out of their car to fight
something that wants to kill them? Meanwhile, I got a message
from you telling me you're afraid, it's getting harder to breathe,
your body's no longer responding to treatment.

3. *We were all in love with Tessie*

Rick Dennis was in love with Tessie Kevin Gibson was in love with
Tessie Lambert was (probably) in love with Tessie Dave Klugman was
(pantingly) in love with Tessie Jean-Guy (with his chocolates) was in
love with Tessie I was ('fangirl') in love with Tessie Bryan Burke (in
his 'Brian Burke' way) was in love with Tessie Fletcher was in love
with Tessie (though maybe it was the idea of Tessie Fletcher was in
love with) Bobby P was in (a) love (that spilled-puddles-at-her-feet-
and-in-their-reflections-he-saw-his-own-curly-fro) with Tessie but
Wayne Krill was (the most) in love and the last one to love her besides
Kaiden, her son, who right this moment is in love with Tessie.

YOUR BODY IS A CASINO

Feel that gnaw? Your body's sweet to the dark vermin today,
their main course in an all-you-can-eat free buffet open 24/7
so you have to wonder how much weight will you lose this time,
sickness ordering shots from a cocktail waitress, jangling money
in your face, knows power is a winner's game. You lose your chips
but it's part of the deal, all these people stepping around the mess
as you lay beating on the steam-cleaned floor. *Where's the fucking
emergency door?* You ask me how I got so smart, well I ordered room
service two months ago – do you think they let me laze about waiting?
Life is full of spectacle, you must learn to love bloodshot so you can
look yourself in the eye. I learned long ago that gambling's about fear
and innocence, odds are you're not the worst off in the room, but still
when the cleaners come they breathe into their collars, the stench
like nothing they've ever known: call it vermin belch. It's a bust.

BAROMETRIC PRESSURE CHANGES

Windsock strain, tumbled trellis, ripped bamboo – if I try to tell
you about the wind one word swallows the next, I am gasping, it
was Wednesday my illness is back, I lost myself in a barking dog I
mean went down a tunnel, came back the moment I left, a snap a
blink, the darkest heart of a galling wind, my head somewhere near
to that, dancing on a pile of disease. The compounded balderdash
of wind, it was Friday, where was my lover? Where was I? the bed
the sticky notes and philosophical books trying to hide from the
clamour of wind – sent texts because I could not speak, the outside
vibrating the sound of my voice, the dog's bark fierce stupor then
vicious blank, my lover in the city shouting we say no to nuclear
dump! his banner slapped by claps of wind, the raging >REPEAT<
the raging wind infinitum, wind-sneering wind-sucked the mother
chucker wind~

> so I've decided to be a muse of quiet suffering
> pale skin slumped in a blanket-nest and muumuu-
> wrapped, now more wind than water, than blood
> a sculpture made from waiting for tomorrow
> trying to rest in a rush – hush: there's hurry.

THE WEATHER

1. It's back, settling in like an old friend, so even though I'm angry and scared I somehow want to embrace it. Does that make me a narcissist? A romantic? I say to illness: *Hey you – it's been a long time.*

2. Seven years, I'm softer now. I will sink into my bed more deeply. Dash will have to flip the mattress every couple of weeks. I will sink more readily. Illness replies: *I have missed the boundaries of your body.*

3. More and more my dog hides under our bed, afraid of the weather. It's either old age or climate change. He takes pills to counter one of them.

4. Today I read the beginning of someone else's story: *The disease has been in remission seven years.* I see no point in lying to you, this is all true. A good story is a body with so many elements working together. I look out the window and the wind has stopped. But then it blows again, stronger.

5. The wind has severed limbs from trees, driven me mad for three days. It might be the cause of all of this, sharp noise spinning me out, the barometric pressure, the world devouring itself and the build-up of its Earth-burp, like when a hanger falls to the ground, my son hits a high note, when I flush the toilet, plastic crinkling, a door lock clicking, the sound of my own voice when I speak.

6. My acupuncturist needled me in my bed today, showed me where to press on the bottom of my feet to get rid of fear – *fear feeds the illness*. I'm frightened if I touch it too much and stop being afraid I'll lose the desire to write – *fear feeds the writing*.

7. I am sheltered on a couch in my brick box office, surrounded by poetry and memoir, books about trauma, books about illness, four books on the top shelf about the Rolling Stones, which I'll begin to read as the band members die off, one by one. Or when my father does.

8. I always think about my parents when it comes back. Illness reminds me I'm a daughter.

9. Cicero says that *a room without books is like a body without a soul*. It's quiet out here, away from the house and the people inside it who only want what's best for me. The wind's picked up again. There's a zombie cyclone over Queensland. New South Wales is flooded. I read about a dust storm there too. My illness has come back with a malice I haven't known for seven years. I need to be alone.

10. Each time I cry today I am supremely alone.

11. Everything I write today is mine alone.

12. In America, my brother and his family are loved-up, snowed-in. People there, used to snow, cannot believe the snow. They take selfies of themselves in it, smiling. Thousands have been left without power. Three people have died.

13. When the attack comes it will be a violent storm. I am preparing for it. I am trying to prepare for it. It's annoying because I cannot prepare.

* 'The disease has been in remission seven years' from Sarah Manguso's *The Two Kinds of Decay*

A USEFUL BODY

A USEFUL BODY

1.

I crawled from couch to kitchen
when I stayed home sick from school
afraid a man might look inside
and know I was alone. It was the 80s
in America, kidnapping fashionable
and there was my young, pliable body,
the milk cartons, a single shoe in the street
I thought belonged to a missing girl.

2.

At school in an empty room
a boy pushed me to the ground
said *this is how you do it*
humping his heft onto my body.

His jeans rubbed against mine.

I memorised the patterns in the ceiling.

When I told the teacher who told my parents
and the boy had to say he was sorry
he became my guardian for the rest of year five:

> I was so grateful because it meant
> that no one could mess with me
> anymore.

3.
I'm still scared at night, rarely ride
my bike in the dark even though it's three years
since that man jumped in front of me, my bike light
blinking all over my body while I cowered in the street
(the tram stop / the evening cars cruising by)
– he said he was going to rip me in two

        (and I was so grateful
        that he didn't.)

4.
Once a man broke into my home
and put his hand between my thighs
then climbed out my bedroom window.
Probably one of your friends said the cops,
the beer bottles from a party we'd had
guilty as my thighs.

5.
Such a useful body, magnificent
but sex can be a problem.
Once I was messing around with a man
who I told to stop and he tried and tried
and it was a challenge but eventually he stopped.
Why did you have to play with me like that?
I should've asked him the exact same thing.

6.

Last night I was at a party celebrating the success
of a group of friends and I posed with my arms around two men –
there's him, me, and cleavage one said as we looked at the photo
but I don't remember the image on his phone, it's hard to know
what I remember, but I remember telling a male friend about it
hours later, drinks later, and he moved the collar of my dress
to better see my cleavage.

7.

My daughter is a gymnast, can climb a rope faster
than her two older brothers using only her arms,
legs straight out, pointed toes.
She has such a magnificent, useful body.
She'll be ten in October.

SAFETY

My daughter thinks safety's a right, not an untethered thing over her
head forever trailing shadows. Her world is open, like air, and she
scoops it up by the lungful, so far from my own of glimpsing men
who get off at my stop on the last train home, the fumbled phone
and the rushing pace, obsessive instinct and the hope of a voice on
the other end to guide me through the edged night.

   In her world, there's not a single reason not to love.

She'll grow, her flowering will be mighty and she'll outlast the
 innocence of spring, why I wish on the day of her first bleed I
 could give it to her – safety. I'd wrap it in layers of tissue, precious
 because it's so close to extinction, and she'd bounce it up and
 down in her hand, unsure of what to do with something so calm
 and obvious.

       One day she'll harness her own secrets;
      she'll baffle herself looking in the mirror;
         she'll give off her body's own scent;
       she'll stop climbing trees in sundresses;
         she'll look over her shoulder.

A DISTRIBUTION OF BLOOD

1.

Blood dreams of breaking free. Outside of its walls
is a strange light, and just as the sun calls to children
and walkers, to the drying clothes and the horse in the paddock
to weeds and to surfers and to wide-brimmed hats, so it calls to blood:

take action.

2.

Like fire, blood stinks of red, colour of war
and anger, colour of love. Blood hungers,
often on the hunt when nothing's to be found,

knowing there is no such thing as nothing.

3.

There's no innocence in red, goddamnit. That flew away
with the image of the apple, the rose, the devil's tail
and the high heels, the red dress

the walk home.

4.

Once blood shows itself it tends to flow.
If left un-bandaged, rivers can run through suburbs
making housewives scream, and when the men drive home
from their offices through the flood of it, they feel uncomfortable.
The blood only dries out on the long skirts of the desert a few hours away
where bananas are sold with black spots on the peel

if they're sold at all.

5.

Blood stains, pushes its way
through every fibre like a diva.
It sings arias, and sometimes death metal.
Afternoons, while menstruating, there is a natural folk vein.

Or jazz. Or blues.

NO LONGER A 10 (OR 'FUCK YOU, TRUMP')

Tepid water & chalk smells

my very breath & sweat

the seethe of good condensation

the packed domesticity of my body

hurried & morning burn-burn

moving kilos like crammed earth

piled before my tennis shoes

half way up I go down again

talking mirrors make heavy words

strong as I'll be for the rest of the day

strong as I'll be for the rest of the day

> not like I'm asking the audience to whistle
>
> or bring me an Ugg boot filled with Chandon,
>
> not like I'm asking for more hours in the day.

SOUS CHEF

This is how I remember you: Thursday nights, stray curls
strong arms, beads & masks, stretch pants, your brown skin
        so light and warm
        I think it melts
        in fractions.

On Thanksgiving you made empanadas.
Next to you I was useless while trying to help, a tissue waiting
for someone to pluck me up & blow. Your children petted the dog,
their bodies like caramel-pops, why the dog licked them so intently.
Those kids got their good manners & feist from you and I miss you,
message through seventeen time zones

                    to ask how you are.

Tired of pushing the boulder uphill looking for flat land.

Rumour has it the top of the hill is rocky & the other side steep
so the boulder will roll out of control, crushing the second gens below –
it's gravity, scary shit, which is why I'm saying I'd be calmer
if those in power learned to cook like you

              with culture birthed
           from the gut of the earth
               a masher to keep
                the hands busy
             flesh for them to feel.

REFUGE

On the walk to the seven-day supermarket:
boarded windows next to broken windows of closed shops
and scarf-starers averting their eyes with closed minds –

everything's *closed*. The children hold her hand.
They walk everywhere together, thinking separately.
This is what love has made. This is what they call themselves.

She remembers old things, language and land.
When the post comes, she hates that the package
has been tampered with, the soft letter inside changed.

Last night's discussion was the fire, earlier death-in-custody.
There is an endpoint, though it's so far off she's lost the horizon
and the waves are wracking her boat.

The faces are in her dreams, like clocks, racing her.
When she buys an orange, they're everywhere. They're on TV
and in the car next to her. She sees them at the planetarium, on the beach.

At least she has her house and her god, which are almost identical;
she has the sky and her feet, which touch. At night she lay the book
of poems on her chest   *and opens   and opens   and*

NOT A SONNET ABOUT GOLFING

Nothing is missing. The outside won't match no matter who you are.
(Some people wish they'd been born animals; is that any stranger
than wishing you'd never been born at all?) You might make odd sounds
when cold or scared but also music when you mate, if you like to fornicate.

Nothing is strange if nothing is normal & nothing is missing
if you look for it. Take these two eyes in their endless business
& place them above the knowing mouth that understands silence
& how the dam might burst & let there be fresh water

because nothing is missing; hands are for touching
scientists don't need to tell us that & minds are for thinking
or hadn't you thought of that? Some people wish
they'd been born someone else but someone else is wrong.

We are all a hole in one.
We all make music when we come.

TRANSLATION

orange sash
bent over
toward him
this is his
green trees
clouds shrouding
Western
& transformed
as I
drip of my
my children
w/out
his iphone
of his hands

in the shade
folded knees
at the temple
meditation
scented with
mountaintops
lives
1:30
wipe the slick
hair w/ mod-
tiptoeing
distracting
sacred world
blessed message

bald head
we're walking
hush: praying
laudable
sky dew
over small
transported
in the afternoon
of my skin
esty shawl
closer & passing
we note
in the palm
be the text

FRANZ SCHUBERT & GEORGIE FAME LYING DOWN TOGETHER INSIDE OF ME

Once I'd ordered the French wine, the old drunk
in and out of the café until at last he tried to steal a bike
arguing with the waiters – *finally* Icelandic,
English the sun that hides this city's moon –
I thought I'd write about the live installation,
the five pianos topped with champagne and beer,
pastries and grapes, chocolates and cheeses
and the five players and the five singers
performing 'An die Musik' un-   simultaneously,
how it made me laugh, I told every person near me
I'm so happy until I cried, but not even imported
Bordeaux could uncover the words so smothered
by the feel of it, beauty the chaos of our tiny lives.

Later I met with a woman from the conference,
her hair still damp from soaking in a hot spring
and we compared notes on how bodies respond
to overwhelming grandeur, then the Frenchman
she'd met while both in bathers, him twelve years
younger and interested in film, joined us for a couple
more drinks, told us the story of exactly how he'd got here.

I could tell you how he looked away when I spoke,
sat with his shoulder touching hers, but I'd be admitting
I felt old. Meanwhile, eating hotdogs on the way
to the jazz club, I felt, for a moment, like a kid.

I ordered beer brewed locally, it didn't matter
though I thought everything was supposed to matter,
like when they kissed beside me, they were either in a movie
or high school, that's how long it lasted, that's how much
it mattered, but I was full from the drinks and the hotdog
and I tried to appear nonchalant, thinking about travelling
and wondering if it makes me a different person
when the quartet started playing 'Sunny' – the name
of my sick child back home, how he touches my cheek
when I tell him I'm sorry – and hand in hand my companions
left me, lost in the song, just like at the museum again,
I'm so happy until I cried, chaos the beauty of our wild lives.

KISS

I.

The child in golden pyjamas sleeps
with open curtains so morning is nothing
but sun, in the summer's night-paste
her sheets thrown off, looking to the ceiling
as if to a stage, moon-lit role-play
where she is the high voice, also the low
she kisses the back of her hand :

> : lips rough on smooth skin because she picks them
> raw, puckered, a slow-rolling head finding motion
> without any reason, something hers & secret
> thinks she's never heard the crickets so loud
> before tonight, how they move their legs
> now moving hers, thinks she is guilty
> of falling in love.

(You saw your parents kiss, tried to kiss them in that way, the deep
  intake of breath, the flaring nostrils, eyes closed, them telling
  you to stop, laughing shortly & appalled, you wanting to cry but
  holding it in like a stolen trinket in your pocket, them laughing
  longer, later, in bed, after they'd nearly kissed each other's faces
  off.)

2.

& role-play with the girl
she never knows is black
until the girl tells her so
you don't actually think my dad's white
can mean anything when so much is pretend
  pretend white barbie dolls with feet
  for high heels & short short shorts
  the sticky stick legs & arms, kissing closed-mouth
  girl on girl, until they fly, floating over houses
  & orange carpet, you should see their smiles
  when they land on that pretend island :
        : theirs like barbies' are hard in the dark
        though soft when they let go
        either way, the red beat
      between her thighs, the ache for time
      to pass now, bring her true love
      bring her breasts.

(You watched enough TV to know that the best kisses are long kisses
& because it was the 80s they were all lips crushing lips so that is
what you knew & that is what you did & that is how you dreamed.)

3.
She doesn't remember them talking
what they said, how they knew
only Jeremy wearing a brown jacket
shiny & puffy, cream stripe across
his chest, jeans are stiff & navy blue
sure does smile sweetly, all him
four square & jump ropes have nothing
to do with *Jeremy* :

> : they kiss behind the smokestack
> his lips closing over the metal
> & wire & rubberband of his mouth
> can't stop thinking are they cutting him
> is there blood, remembers to remember
> how the winter air feels on her cheeks
> something about warmth & steam.

(Yes there might have been too many VC Andrews books hiding
in your closet but did you kiss your cousin or was it your brother
after they compared notes on pubic hair, *I have it there*, *I do too*, the
dank stink, the dirty feel, you wished your parents would just come
home.)

4.

How did she get inside the closet
things are expected there, a friend
is witness outside the closet, listening
for tongues, he'll send a report to school
next day & now the darkness
pushing against her in all of the places
the boy leaves alone, claustrophobic energy :

                                : their tongues lost & persistent
                            smash of teeth, it's wet & confused
                                a new language, an awkward
                            animal, the next teenage suburban.

(You thought if you kissed him he'd like you so you kissed him & he
didn't.)

5.
Cigarettes, cigarettes & lighters
her image nothing like her, all smoke
& mirrors & movie screens, magazines
that little voice sobbing inside
the only redhead she'll ever kiss
hard-rock freckles & hands the hands
        the *hands* the *hands* :

                : they taste of waste, dangerous
                   & lazy, something empty
             for their full-mouthed tongues
                  she loosens, tenses, wild
             & afraid of herself, wondering
             what would her parents think

(It started with a kiss: *kiss & make it better, kiss the pain away, kiss the ring, a kissing stone, kiss my feet, kiss my ass, kiss a frog, kiss & make up, kiss & tell, sealed with a kiss, kiss the sky, kiss Jimi Hendrix & his long kiss goodnight, kiss of death, kiss it goodbye, kiss me like you mean it.*)

6.

Naked & alone in a single bed, music playing
through the night, but when he sleeps with her
after the break-in, *sleeps* with her, clothed
with denim-rough creases, in the morning
she touches the Levi snap's indentation
in the small of her back, then rain for two weeks
their dense space until that Tuesday afternoon first kiss :

: her heart beats higher
than her chest
her heart is almost
in her throat
no breath
just tongue
tongue & lips
the snap of immortality
open-eyed kissing
music playing
through the night.

(You couldn't stop kissing & after he left you your lips kept going,
unsure of what to do now that his kissing had stopped, unsure of
who you are if kissing ever stops, so friends, strangers, they all tasted
the same.)

7.
The haze of it, Knob Creek whisky
& stubs of Camel Lights, stereo set
on shelves of milk crates & bricks
Otis Redding, gap-toothed 24 year
old girl who smells like saguaros
in summer's bloom :

: like kissing herself, who she wants to be
adult & risky, high-brow art
the painting at MoMA worth stealing
slippery boundary of body & tongue
kissing her & her kissing her
& now what will your parents think

(You wondered if the compulsion to kiss was due to love or the
compulsion to love was because of a kiss, you searched books, pubs,
media, the streets & you *watched* kissing, *tried* kissing, sometimes
the strings of saliva screaming that it served-you-right, sometimes a
warm bed, sometimes a home, maybe a dog sleeping next to the bed.)

8.
Love before the kiss, like reverse psychology
ancient before it's new, wise before it's born
never too old for a good trick like this
what is it called – the self-engendering
of two lovers moving toward a kiss :

                                              : can it go on & on & on

(She swallowed him, tasting of the ocean & like the velvety
underbelly of a stingray brushing her bare legs kicking in a sluggish
rhythm, he took her by surprise, made her reflect on chance & living
as if she could die, he was the water & the sky, all or nothing, always
all, she couldn't explain how a love grows except for this – when she
swallowed the ocean, tasting of him, coral reefs covered her eyes &
sea monkeys took harbour in her body, she gave each one a name.)

ALWAYS EVERYTHING

Love, another time in a foreign city we held hands all weekend.
A tram almost hit me but you pulled me in. We laughed
as it flew past, ringing its bell. It was like a movie.

Love is vexed except when it is not, and often it is not.
Sometimes it's like a hot road melting tyres, or a thick novel
under a bedside lamp with a bookmark stuck in the middle.

I used to dream of you when I was young and read fairy tales
and now that I've had a gutful of presidents and prime ministers
I dream of you even more. Let's turn off the news

and crawl under covers, make our own headlines spark with stink.
Ring the smoke alarms! Howl the dog! and in the morning
let's cook eggs. The world is still us.

Acknowledgements

Some of these poems or earlier versions of them were first published in the chapbook *Thump: and other poems*, Garron Press 2017. 'Trying to Write about Ménière's' was published in the anthology *Shaping the Fractured Self: Poetry of Chronic Illness and Pain*, UWAP 2017. 'A Useful Body' was published in *#MeToo: Stories from the Australian Movement*, Pan Macmillan 2019.

Thanks to the editors of the following journals for publishing these poems, or earlier versions of them: *Australian Poetry Journal*; *Bellevue Literary Journal* (USA); *Cordite*; *foam:e*; *From our Desk: Poet's Corner Anthology*; *Griffith Review*; *Grow, Grow, Grow Your Own Almanac*; *Island*; *Monstering* (USA); *The Crows in Town: Newcastle Poetry Prize Anthology 2017*; *Soft Serve: Newcastle Poetry Prize Anthology 2019*; *Plumwood Mountain*; *Rabbit*; *Rochford Street Review*; *Saltbush Review*; *Social Alternatives*; *Wordgathering* (USA).

Thank you to Nasty Women of Words for publishing 'Safety' on your website as a response to Donald Trump's enraging election, and to the judges of the Charles Rischbieth Jury Poetry Prize for naming 'Freefall' a runner-up. 'Man & Man, Man & Ape, Ape & Ape & Women' was showcased in the art exhibition *This Breath is not Mine to Hold*, and thank you to the JM Coetzee Centre for Creative Practice for allowing me to audit the special Coetzee course, which inspired the poem. The final stanza in 'Kiss' is also a stanza in the poem 'Sea Monkeys' in *Rhymes with Hyenas* because I never thought 'Sea Monkeys' would be published.

Thanks to Susy Kelly for her completely cool collage work on the cover, and to Melinda Bufton, Michelle Cahill and Peter Boyle for not only their kind endorsements but also their poetry. Thanks to Michael Bollen for continuing to foster and support Australian poetry. I'm honoured to be published by Wakefield Press and thrilled about keeping it local, which also leads to thanking the organisers of local readings – Halifax, No Wave and Spoke-n-Slurred – for encouraging my work. I love Adelaide and its poetry scene. Great gratitude to top readers and life-long friends Alison Flett, Cassie Flanagan-Willanski and Rachael Mead and, as always and endlessly, big love to Dash, Guthrow, Sunny, Matilda and our dog Tom.

Wakefield Press is an independent publishing and
distribution company based in Adelaide, South Australia.
We love good stories and publish beautiful books.
To see our full range of books, please visit our website at
www.wakefieldpress.com.au
where all titles are available for purchase.
To keep up with our latest releases, news and events,
subscribe to our monthly newsletter.

Find us!

Facebook: www.facebook.com/wakefield.press
Twitter: www.twitter.com/wakefieldpress
Instagram: www.instagram.com/wakefieldpress

Printed in Australia
AUHW020048071122
371187AU00010B/37

9 781743 059623